THE ADVENTURE COLLECTION

SOLO PIANO

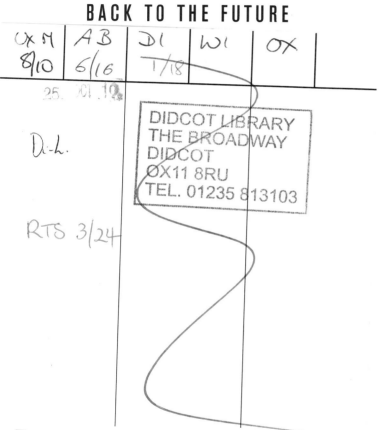

WISE PUBLICATIONS
part of The Music Sales Group
London / New York / Paris / Sydney / Copenhagen / Berlin / Madrid / Tokyo

Back To The Future
(Theme)
Composed by Alan Silvestri

3

The Beach
(The Beach Theme – Swim To Island)

Composed by Angelo Badalamenti

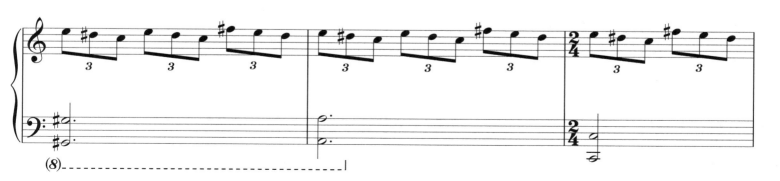

9

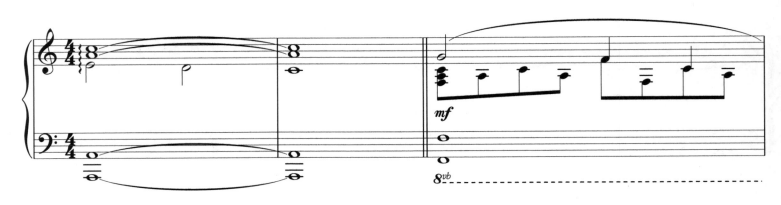

Butch Cassidy
And The Sundance Kid
(The Sundance Kid)

Composed by Burt Bacharach

The Goonies
(Theme)

Composed by Dave Grusin

First Knight
(Arthur's Fanfare / Promise Me)

Composed by Jerry Goldsmith

21

The Hunt For Red October
(Hymn To Red October)

Composed by Basil Poledouris

23

25

Jurassic Park
(Theme)
Composed by John Williams

28

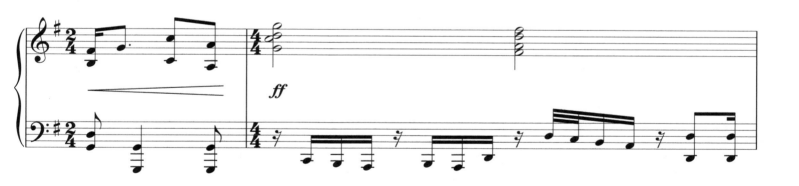

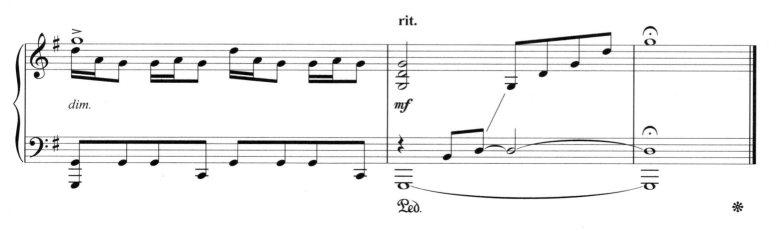

King Kong
(A Fateful Meeting)

Composed by James Newton Howard

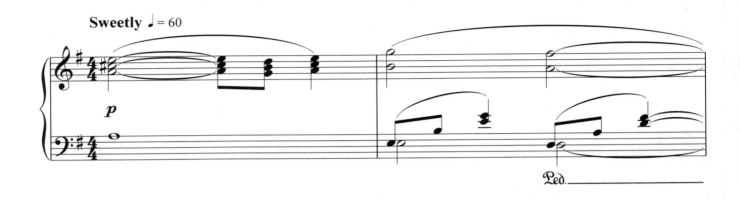

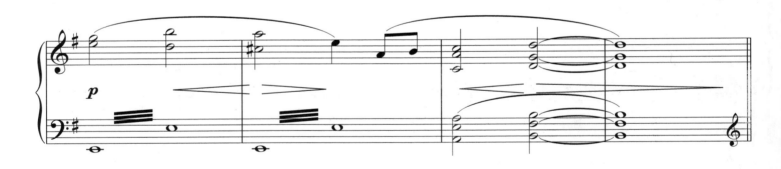

A Knight's Tale
(St. Vitus' Dance)

Composed by Carter Burwell

The Last Of The Mohicans

(Main Title)

Composed by Trevor Jones

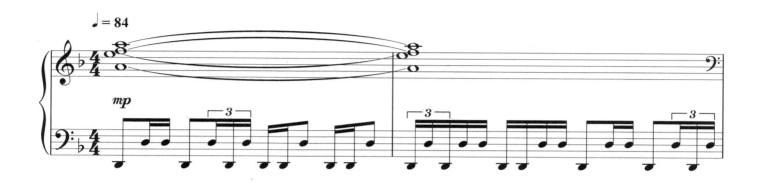

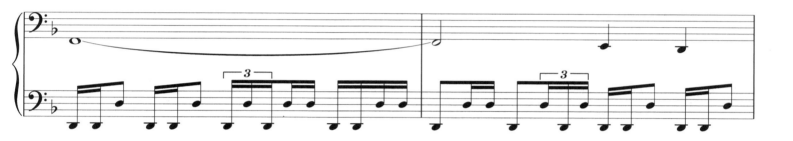

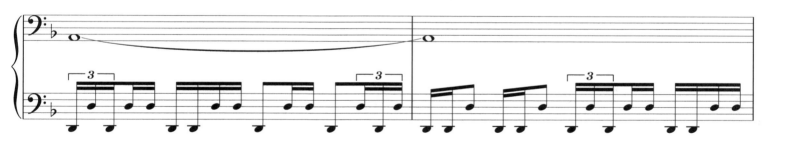

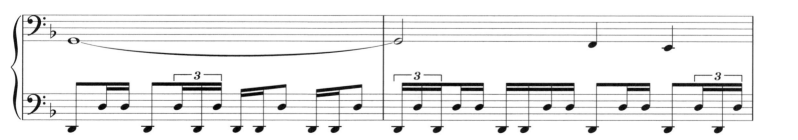

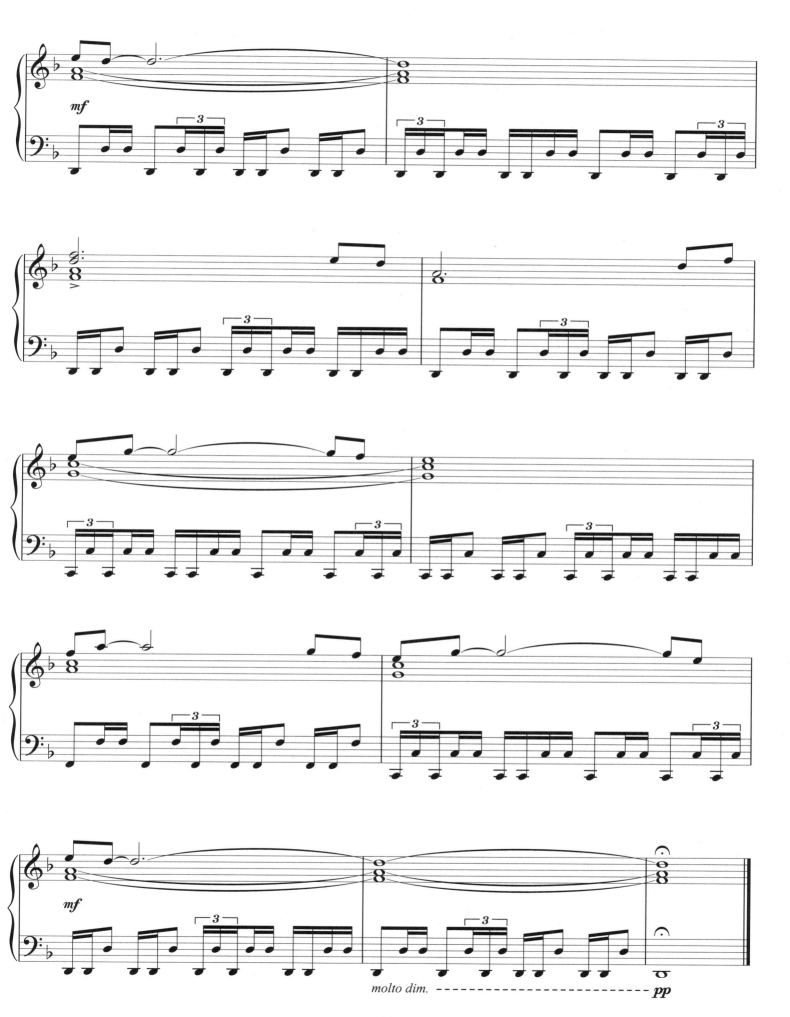

Lara Croft Tomb Raider:
The Cradle Of Life
(Pandora's Box)

Composed by Alan Silvestri

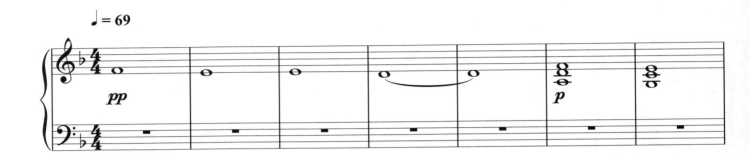

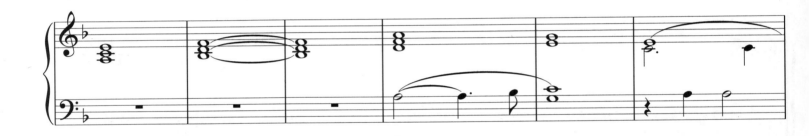

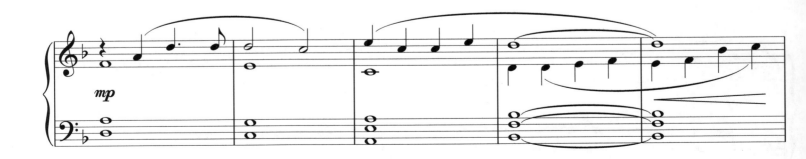

Lawrence Of Arabia
(Main Title)

Composed by Maurice Jarre

poco accel.

cresc.

a tempo

f

mp

alla con fuoco

molto rit.

49

Legends Of The Fall
(The Ludlows)

Composed by James Horner

The Man In The Iron Mask

(Heart Of A King)

Composed by Nick Glennie-Smith

The Mask Of Zorro

(Zorro's Theme)

Composed by James Horner

60

The Mummy
(The Sand Volcano)

Composed by Jerry Goldsmith

The Mummy Returns

(The Mummy Returns)

Composed by Alan Silvestri

National Treasure
(National Treasure Suite / Ben / Treasure)

Composed by Trevor Rabin

70

Pirates Of The Caribbean:
The Curse Of The Black Pearl
(Will And Elizabeth)

Composed by Klaus Badelt

73

Plunkett & Macleane
(Rebecca)

Composed by Craig Armstrong

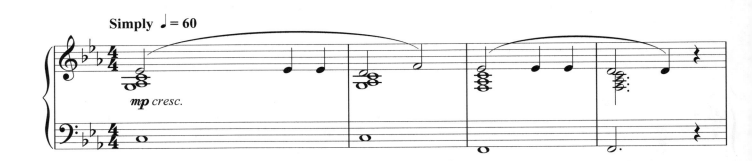

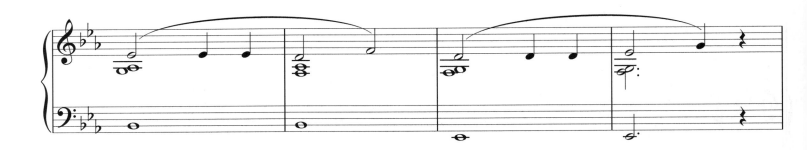

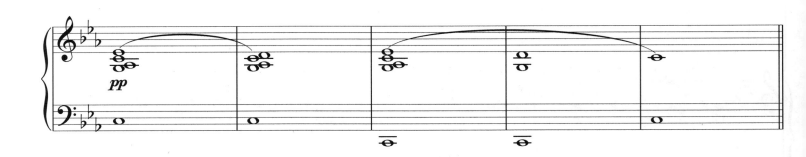

The Princess Bride
(A Happy Ending)

Composed by Mark Knopfler

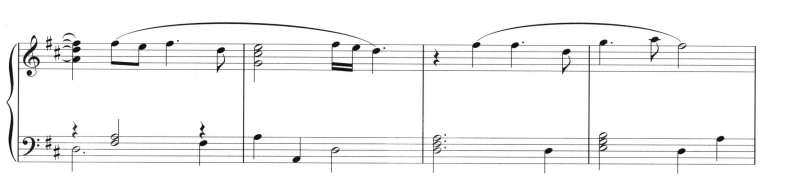

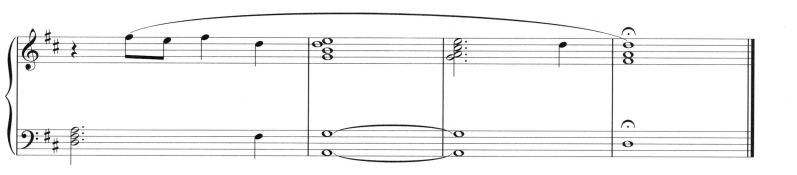

Raiders Of The Lost Ark

(Raiders March)

Composed by John Williams

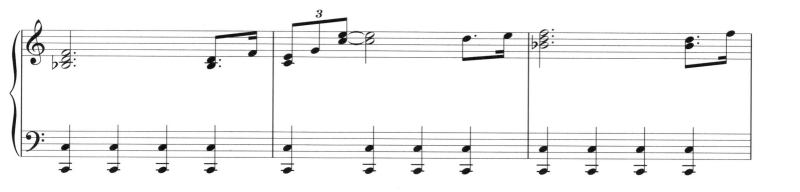

Robin Hood: Prince Of Thieves
(Marian At The Waterfall)
Composed by Michael Kamen

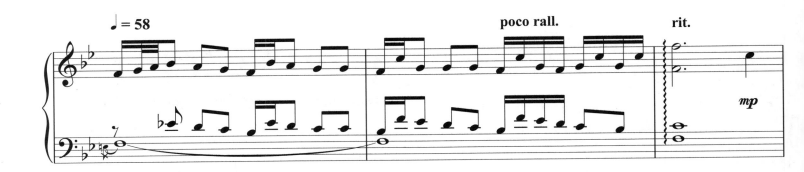

Romancing The Stone
(End Credits Theme)
Composed by Alan Silvestri

Sahara
(Ironclad)
Composed by Clint Mansell

The Three Musketeers
(D'Artagnan (Galliard & Air))

Composed by Michael Kamen

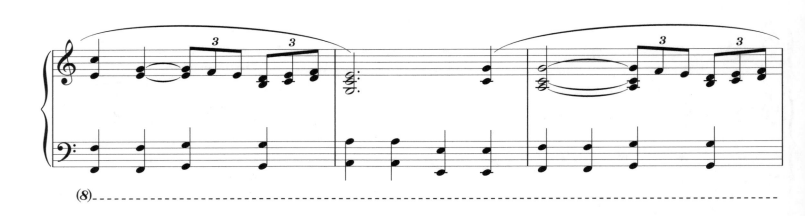

(8)- -

(8)- -

(8)- -

(8)- ⌐

8vb- - ⌐

1 2 3 4 5 6 7 8 9

Published by
Wise Publications
14-15 Berners Street, London W1T 3LJ, UK.

Exclusive Distributors:
Music Sales Limited
Distribution Centre, Newmarket Road, Bury St Edmunds, Suffolk IP33 3YB, UK.
Music Sales Pty Limited
120 Rothschild Avenue, Rosebery, NSW 2018, Australia.

Order No. AM989428
ISBN 978-1-84609-946-5
This book © Copyright 2007 Wise Publications,
a division of Music Sales Limited.

Edited by Fiona Bolton.
New music arrangements by Derek Jones.
Music processed by Paul Ewers Music Design.
Cover design by Michael Bell Design.
Compiled by Nick Crispin.
Printed in the EU.

Your Guarantee of Quality
As publishers, we strive to produce every book to the highest commercial standards.
This book has been carefully designed to minimise awkward page turns and to make playing from it a real pleasure.
Particular care has been given to specifying acid-free, neutral-sized paper made from
pulps which have not been elemental chlorine bleached.
This pulp is from farmed sustainable forests and was produced with special regard for the environment.
Throughout, the printing and binding have been planned to ensure a sturdy,
attractive publication which should give years of enjoyment.
If your copy fails to meet our high standards, please inform us and we will gladly replace it.

www.musicsales.com

This publication is not authorised for sale in
the United States of America and / or Canada

LOOK OUT
FOR THESE OTHER
GREAT TITLES IN
THE MUSIC
FROM THE MOVIES
SERIES

THE ACTION COLLECTION
AM984038

THE ANIMATION COLLECTION
AM984027

THE FILM NOIR COLLECTION
AM984005

THE HORROR COLLECTION
AM984016

THE SCI-FI COLLECTION
AM983983